Looking Good

FOR GUYS

by Douglas Altman

Rourke Publications, Inc.
Vero Beach, FL 32964

The author wishes to thank the following people for their help in the preparation of this book:

Eileen Griffin for her work on the illustrations in this book. Ms. Griffin is an artist, illustrator and the owner of a graphic arts company.

Dixie Montgomery, owner and director of a modeling school and agency.

Library of Congress Cataloging-in-Publication Data

Altman, Douglas, 1961-
   Grooming for guys / Douglas Altman.
       p.   cm. — (Looking good)
   Bibliography: p.
   Includes index.
   Summary: Gives advice on cleanliness, diet, exercise, clothes, and other aspects of good grooming.
   1. Grooming for boys—Juvenile literature. [1. Grooming.] I. Title. II. Series: Looking good (Vero Beach, Fla.)
RA777.2.A47   1989   88-20958
646.7′044—dc 19   CIP
ISBN 0-86625-284-3   AC

CONTENTS

YOUR BODY
KEEPING UP THE MACHINE

Let's start from the inside. Fact, unhealthy people generally don't look good. If what's going on inside your body is ugly, then how can you expect to look any better on the outside?

Exercise

What we're talking about here are **exercise** and **eating habits.** Exercise is an important part of staying healthy, as everyone in the world has probably told you already. This doesn't mean you should work out on exercise machines till you drop; it just means that you should spend a little time each day reminding your heart and your lungs how they're supposed to work. That's called *aerobic exercise.* Anything that keeps your body in constant steady motion is aerobic exercise — swimming and jogging, for instance. Ball sports, like soccer or football, can be aerobic too, provided you're not the kind of player who stands around waiting for something to happen.

If you don't exercise, and would much rather sit and watch TV, then you are becoming what is commonly referred to as a "Couch Potato" (or "Video Potato," if you rent lots of movies). If you think that's an attractive thing to be, perhaps you should go into your kitchen and take a good look at a potato. Ugly sucker, isn't it?

Diet

Having good eating habits means following your common sense. Does it make sense to have a double-dip hot-fudge sundae just before dinner? No, not really. Does it make sense to eat six enormous portions of Grandma's fantastic

4

spaghetti, even though you were full after the second portion? No, I don't think so. Does it make sense to eat peanut butter and jelly sandwiches for breakfast, lunch, and dinner *every* day of the week because you like them so much? Think again.

Eat normal sized portions and space your eating throughout the day. Go easy on the sweets, and vary the kinds of foods you eat. *Never* let yourself get so starved that you'll eat anything.

The four basic food groups are:

> Meats and fish
>
> Milk products
>
> Breads and cereals
>
> Fruits and vegetables

The four food groups provide your body with these nutrients: protein, fat, carbohydrates, vitamins, and minerals. Add water, and you have a list of the basic nutrients *everyone* needs. A well balanced diet means you get the right portions of these four basic food groups daily.

If you're overweight it could be because of a poor diet and lack of exercise, but not always. If you *feel* you have good eating habits, and get enough exercise, but still tend to be overweight, see a doctor. Whatever you do, don't go on crash diets all by yourself. Most diets that aren't prescribed by a doctor are hard on your body, and some can actually cause you to *gain* weight. If you starve yourself all day, and eat one big meal at night to lose weight, you may end up gaining weight rather than losing it!

6

Vitamin and Mineral Needs for Teenage Boys

Vitamin/Mineral	Daily Need	Source	Why Needed
Calcium	1,000-1,200 mg	Dairy products	Bone formation Healthy teeth
Iron	18 grams	Liver, red meat, raisins	Red blood cell production
Vitamin A	5,000 International Units	Green/yellow vegetables: carrots, tomatoes, cheese	Good vision Bone/teeth formation
Vitamin D	400 IU	Fish, sunlight, egg yolks, fortified milk	Healthy heart Healthy nervous system
Vitamin E	12-15 IU's	Milk, eggs, fish, meats, cereals, nuts, vegetables	Red blood cell production
Vitamin K	5-100 mg	Spinach, bran, rice, tomatoes	Blood coagulation
Vitamin B1 (Thiamine)	Approx. 1 mg	Pork, beef, liver, whole or enriched grains, beans	Healthy nervous system
Vitamin B2 (Riboflavin)	1-1.5 mg	Milk, liver, enriched cereals, cheese	Red blood cell formation
Vitamin B3 (Niacin)	14-20 mg	Meat, peanuts, enriched grains	Healthy nervous system, brain function
Vitamin B6 (Pyroxine)	2 mg	Corn, wheat germ, lean meats, bananas	Helps reduce cramps Promotes healthy skin
Folic Acid	400 mg	Green leafy vegetables, asparagus, liver, kidneys	Formation of red blood cells
Vitamin B12	3 mg	Lean meat, milk, eggs, cheese, liver	Promotes growth Improves concentration
Vitamin C	45 mg	Citrus fruits, tomatoes, cabbage, potatoes, broccoli, strawberries	Heals wounds Strengthens blood vessels Helps ward off infection

Six Good Reasons to Keep Clean

If you're still not completely convinced of the benefits of good hygiene, maybe you should consider what happens when you have bad hygiene:

You look dirty. With seven layers of skin on your body, you don't need several more layers of dirt on top.

You smell dirty. Even if you don't look dirty, you're at the age where your body can smell pretty ripe if you don't keep clean. Even if you can't smell yourself, everyone else will.

You could aggravate acne conditions. Your body secretes oils that catch dirt and the dirt clogs pores on your skin. That can cause an evil case of zits. Unless you want your face to bear a close resemblance to the moon, you'd better keep clean.

You'll have dental problems. No one likes going under the dentist's drill, but if you don't keep your teeth clean, you may end up having so many fillings, you'll set off the metal detectors at your local airport.

You'll have bad breath. Bad breath is called **halitosis,** and it's the best way to make long distance even *better* than being there. If you have breath that could melt cheese, you probably won't be too popular.

You'll get sick more often. If you're dirty, it means lots of bacteria live on your body, which means lots of bacteria get *into* your body, which means you'll get sick more often. Being sick is no fun — even if you *do* get to stay home and watch reruns of your favorite show.

KEEPING THE MACHINE CLEAN

Let's face it; the days of chocolate-covered faces and mud-covered hands are gone. If you want to look good a thorough daily washing is a must.

Bathing

Shower at least once a day, either when you wake up, or before bed, or any time you feel you need one. If you're very active and sweat a lot, shower more often. Many teenage boys have oily skin. If you're one of them, avoid the temptation to use harsh soaps. Harsh soaps can further irritate an already troubled skin. Use mild soap and wash more frequently. Use a nail brush to get dirt out from under your finger and toe nails.

Taking Care of Your Teeth

It's important to brush your teeth regularly because it's the best way to ward off tooth decay; it keeps your teeth clean and your breath fresh; and nobody wants to look at a smile that's filled with pieces of yesterday's lunch. Floss daily. Sticking a piece of unwaxed string between your teeth may sound like a strange thing to do, but flossing is the best way to clean food particles from between your teeth.

> **TIP:** When you brush, make sure you reach *all* your teeth. The teeth you don't see are still there.

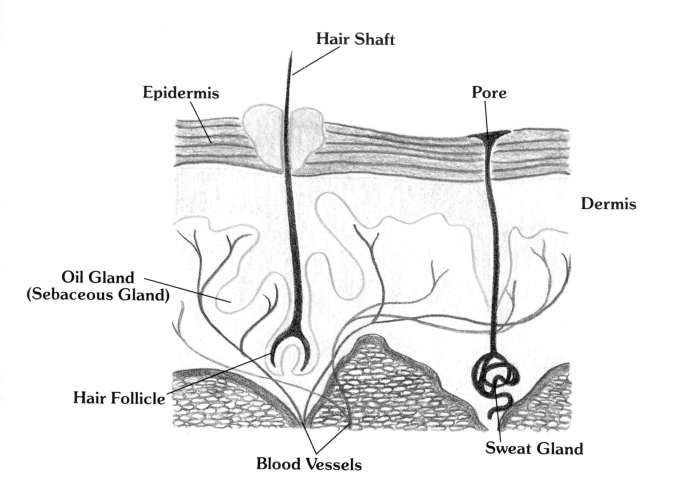

Hair Shaft

Epidermis

Pore

Dermis

Oil Gland
(Sebaceous Gland)

Hair Follicle

Blood Vessels

Sweat Gland

A Word on Acne

Acne is caused by a whole lot of things. Clogged pores, allergic reactions, not washing enough — even over-washing can lead to acne. There are special medications you can use to help clean up zits, but if you've got a bad case, see a special skin doctor called a **dermatologist.**

10

YOUR HAIR

The kind of hair you have is decided by several factors. There's color; blond, red, brown, black and shades in between. There's texture; straight, wavy, curly or kinky. There's thickness and there's density; hair ranges from fine to thick, from thin to full.

Some people have dry hair, which is frizzy and dull-looking; some people have oily hair, which is stringy and limp. There are some people who have "perfect" hair, which is halfway in between too dry and too oily. Very few people have absolutely perfect hair one hundred percent of the time, but you can be close with proper hair care.

Keeping Your Hair Clean

Hair is a net for dirt. It collects dirt better than any other part of your body, so proper hair care is very important. Shampoo two or three times a week. Shampoo more often if your hair is oily or if you use lots of mousse, gels, or hairspray, or you're into sports and you sweat a lot.

Always choose shampoos and conditioners that are right for the kind of hair you have; dry, normal, or oily. When you shampoo, remember you're not just washing your hair, you're washing your scalp; gently rub your scalp with your fingertips while shampooing. Conditioners are designed to replace lost moisture. Condition after you shampoo. For the conditioner to work properly, follow the directions carefully. Most will tell you to work the conditioner in, leave it on for about a minute, and then rinse it out thoroughly. *Remember* — conditioners tend to build up on hair.

Blow-drying

If you blow dry, be careful not to over-dry your hair. Make sure you keep the blower moving; don't keep it on one spot for too long. Avoid using the hottest settings, and don't hold the dryer too close to your head — you don't want to burn your hair. Remember that blow drying tends to straighten hair. If your hair tends to be dry, avoid blow drying; let your hair dry naturally.

> **TIP:** Unless you're grooming your hair into a particular style, you may want to use your fingers instead of a brush when blow drying your hair. Using a brush can straighten and stretch your hair, but using your fingers will help your hair look more natural.

The sun

You must have noticed the effect that the sun has on your hair in the summer; your hair gets sun-bleached. While it might look good, it's not good for you. The sun dries your hair out, removing natural moisturizers. If you spend lots of time out of doors, wear a hat when you can, and condition more often if your hair starts to get dry and brittle. Don't forget the sunscreen for your skin!

Salt water and pool water

The salt of the ocean and chlorine in pools damage hair and skin by drying and thinning it. Make sure you shampoo and condition after you swim.

Hairstyles

Different people look good in different hairstyles. You may find that a style that suits all of your friends makes you look like an absolute geek. Well, don't worry, because there are hairstyles you'll look fantastic in that your friends won't! It's all a matter of finding out what you like. Here are some things to keep in mind when looking for the right hairstyle.

Get your hair cut once every four to six weeks. Hair grows about half an inch each month, and the ends tend to get damaged. Keeping it trimmed will keep it looking better.

Your hairstyle should suit your face. If you have a long face, keep away from styles that pile hair on top. If you have a wide face, keep away from styles that pile hair on the sides. If you have a small head, don't get a butch!

Hair cuts grow out. Yes, even bad hair cuts grow out. It's easy to experiment with different styles until you find one that suits you.

Don't over-do the mousse! A little mousse goes a long way. There are lots of different things you can use in your hair to keep it set a certain way: mousse, gels, cremes, and hairspray. For a long time hair spray was considered uncool for guys, but now it seems to be coming back. I know kids who use things like vaseline to get their hair spiked up. That's not really the best idea. If you've ever had vaseline in your hair, then you know how hard it is to wash out! It's better to use products specifically designed for hair.

14

Don't do anything to your hair that will give your parents a heart-attack! Your parents made me write that.

The type of hair you have defines what you can do with it. If you have very curly hair, then trying to spike it up probably won't work. If you really want to change the texture of your hair, you can get hair relaxers, which straighten your hair, or get a permanent, which curl it. Remember, the chemicals used in perms and straighteners are hard on your hair.

Tips on Brushing

Don't brush your hair when wet; that's when it's weakest.

Don't over-brush if you have oily hair; it stimulates oil glands.

Don't spend 24 hours a day brushing your hair, because there are more important things to do!

Different textures and hair thicknesses require different combs and brushes. Find ones that are right for you. Although it's normal to lose up to 100 hairs a day, you don't want to be pulling them out with a bad brush!

> **TIP:** You don't always need the trendiest hair style to look good. Guys can look good in their plain old basic natural hairstyle, as long as it's clean and neat. It's something to keep in mind if you don't like how the trendiest hairstyles can look on you.

16

YOUR CLOTHES

With your hair and body cared for, now it's time to take a look at some clothes. They say that "clothes make the man." That's not necessarily true, in all honesty "the man makes the man." However, clothes *do* have an effect on how others see us, and how we see ourselves. First let's talk about fabrics.

Fibers and Fabrics

When you look at that annoying tag in the back of your shirt that you always have to tuck down, you'll notice that it tells you what fibers were used in the making of your garment. Most clothes are made of one of the following:

Cotton. Cotton is probably the most common of natural fibers. Cotton is very soft, very comfortable, and *cotton shrinks!*

> **TIP:** If the label does not say pre-shrunk, you can bet if it fits perfectly in the store, it will be too small once you wash it. Always buy a size larger for un-shrunk 100% cotton garments.

Wool. While cotton is a plant, wool is sheep hair. Wool tends to be more expensive than cotton. It is not as soft, and generally needs special care in cleaning — either dry-cleaning or hand washing. Wool is also warmer than cotton, and is worn more often in the winter. Dressy clothes tend to be made of wool.

Silk. Silk is spun by silk worms almost like a spider spins the strands of its web. It is a very fine fiber and weaves into a light-weight, smooth, expensive fabric.

Synthetics. These are man-made fibers, like polyester, dacron, rayon, and nylon. They are generally less expensive than natural fabrics, and they tend to be plastic-looking. Pure polyester clothes are not only hot when you wear them, but are eternally out of style.

Blends. Most clothes you wear are blends of cotton and some synthetic fiber, usually dacron or polyester. Blends tend to feel like cotton, but are less wrinkly, and don't shrink as much.

From Casual to Formal

Just so you know, when people say formal and casual, there are actually rules for what those terms mean.

Casual: Most of what you wear is considered casual — from a bathing suit and T-shirt at the beach, to slacks and a nice sweater for an evening out.

Semi-Formal: This means slacks, a jacket, and a tie, or a matching suit.

Formal: If an invitation says "Formal," you will be expected to wear a tuxedo. If you don't have a tuxedo and can't rent one, you might be able to get away with a dark suit, white shirt and conservative tie.

Expensive doesn't always mean better. Sometimes expensive means you're paying for the name on the label, or even worse, the name of the store. Of course, expensive can also mean you're paying for the quality of merchandise. It's up to you to call the judgement on that one.

If it looks like garbage, it probably is. Look at the stitching, and the quality of the fabric. Are buttons coming off? Are stitches coming out? Are there imperfections in the fabric? Don't buy anything that looks like it was made poorly.

Is it good to follow trends? Yes and no. If you buy all trendy clothes to keep in style, you'll look sharp, but you'll probably pay lots of money for your clothes, and they'll be out of style pretty quickly.

> **TIP:** Trendy clothes tend to be poorly made because the manufacturers want to make them quickly and sell a lot of them before the trend is over.

On the other hand, there are lots of clothes that are fashionable, but outlast trends. "Classic" styles, like jeans, casual slacks and good sweaters are examples. Classic styles are often made better, last longer, and always look good no matter what the current fashion is.

Try it on! Don't assume it will fit because the label says it's your size. Different manufacturers cut garments differently.

The Clothes for You

Models always look good — it's their job to look good, but the simple fact is that not everyone looks good in all the clothes models wear. Different people look better in different types of clothes. The size and shape of your body makes a difference, as well as your skin tone, your hair color, etc. Don't be disappointed if you don't suit the clothes your friends are wearing. As with hairstyles, you're bound to find clothes that look much better on you than on them.

Jean Splicing: a crash course in mixing and matching. Unless you're going for a particularly obnoxious look, you probably want your clothes to match, but matching clothes is a learned skill.

Neutral Colors: White, beige, and gray are neutral — in other words, almost any other color can go well with them. Any shirt that looks good on you would probably go well with either white, gray, or beige pants.

> **TIP:** Remember that blue jeans are considered neutral also: almost any color shirt will go with blue jeans.

Colors that don't match: If your pants and shirt are both of solid colors, you have to find combinations that are pleasing to the eye. In general, green clashes with red, blue clashes with orange, purple clashes with yellow, white clashes with beige. There are an awful lot of exceptions however, because there are so many different shades of colors. The best thing to do is to hold the shirt next to the pants. Does the shirt look better when it's next to the pants, or better when it's by itself?

20

Patterns: Patterned shirts generally call for solid color pants, and patterned pants call for solid shirts. This is because most patterns clash with one another, and even if they don't, your clothes will look too "busy." There should be some color in your patterned shirt that matches the color of your pants. If your pants are pastel blue, for instance, a shirt with the same blue somewhere in the pattern would match.

Be Creative! Just because you buy a shirt to match a particular pair of pants doesn't mean it won't match other things in your wardrobe. There are lots of different ways of mixing and matching to make it seem as though you have more outfits than you really do. You can vary the way you wear your clothes also — wearing shirts out instead of tucked in, for instance.

Layering: This is another way of extending your wardrobe. Layering means putting clothes on top of one another: wearing a solid color T-shirt underneath a patterned button shirt, or wearing a collared shirt beneath a matching sweater. Layering clothes helps keep you warm, and when you're indoors or the weather changes, you can take off the outer layers, and keep looking good down to your T-shirt!

It's uncool to be cold: If the outfit you want to wear is too light for the weather, then don't wear it!

Seasonal clothes: Traditionally, lighter colors, like white and pastels, are worn in the spring and summer. Darker colors and earth tones, like browns, are worn in the fall and winter.

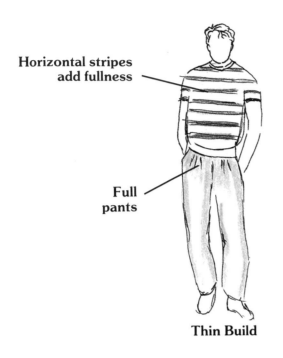

Horizontal stripes add fullness

Full pants

Thin Build

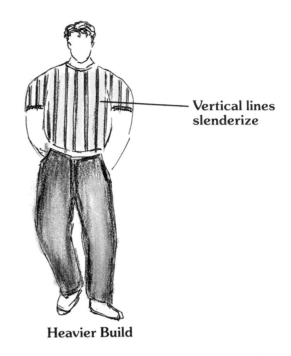

Vertical lines slenderize

Heavier Build

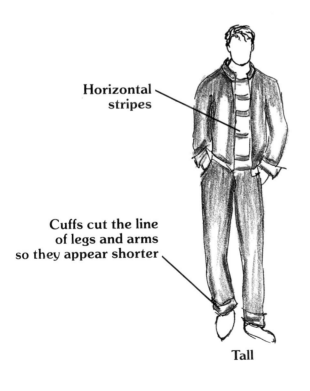

Horizontal stripes

Cuffs cut the line of legs and arms so they appear shorter

Tall

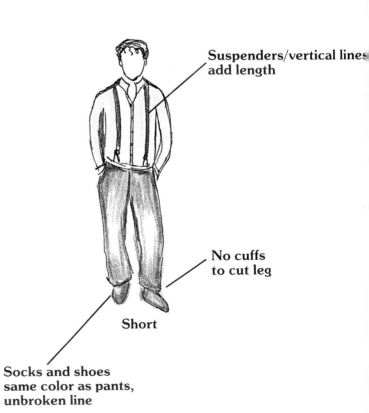

Suspenders/vertical lines add length

No cuffs to cut leg

Short

Socks and shoes same color as pants, unbroken line

22

Using the Illusions

Patterns, colors, and textures create little optical illusions that you can use to beef-up your appearance. Clothes can help you look taller, shorter, broader, or thinner. Here are some suggestions to help you choose what's right for you.

These things make you look thinner:

Cool colors, solid colors, small patterns, smooth fabrics, vertical stripes, thin ties, suspenders.

These things make you look heavier:

Warm colors, light colors, rougher textures, horizontal stripes, vests, wide belts. If you're heavy, tight clothes make you look heavier.

These things make you look taller:

Small patterns, vertical lines, smooth textures and soft fabrics. Jackets that match your pants (matching sweat jackets or denim jackets, for instance), thin ties, suspenders.

These things make you look shorter:

Heavy fabrics, horizontal lines, large patterns, cuffs on pants and sleeves, wide belts, vests, loose-fitting clothes.

Items like jackets and sweaters have some magical effects! If you're overweight, sweaters and jackets can sometimes hide it. If you're thin, the right sweaters and jackets could help you look broader. Vests and half-shirts can help you look broader-chested.

24

Sports Jackets

Every well dressed male should have at least one sports jacket or suit to wear when the need arises. Sports jackets can be worn with dress shirts and nice slacks, or they can be worn more casually, over T-shirts, with jeans. They can make the simplest of outfits fit for a night out.

When you buy a sports jacket remember:

The collar should lie flat against the back of your neck — it shouldn't stick out.

Your arms shouldn't dangle ridiculously out of the sleeves.

The jacket should be long enough to cover your rear end completely.

There are two styles for sports jacket sleeves; you can have the underlying shirt sleeve not show at all, or the shirt sleeve should be three-eighths of an inch longer than the jacket sleeve (which is standard for suits).

When you try on dress slacks, wear the shoes you plan to wear with them. The hem should touch the top of the shoe creating a break in the crease, a few inches up.

TIP: However you dress, you should put your own taste and personality into it. Some clothes may not look good on you simply because they don't suit your personality. Have the guts to wear what you want to wear, don't always be a slave to fashion!

THE TRIMMINGS

In addition to major garments, there are other things guys wear to add to their appearance. They are called accessories. Although accessories are not as large as major pieces of clothing, they can have a dramatic effect on your appearance.

Hats

A stylish cap that matches a major article of clothing can really look sharp! Painters caps and Italian bicycle racing caps are currently in favor. If you feel particularly daring and like to set trends, experiment with different types. Your friends will either think you're incredibly weird, or too cool for words!

Glasses

Everyone knows the "cool" image sunglasses can give. If this is the image you want, then feel free to wear them — but remember the proper places and times. Don't wear them in class because it annoys teachers no end. Don't wear them at night because it's dangerous, and they look silly. Keep in mind that it's hard for people to carry on a conversation with you when they can't see your eyes. If you wear prescription glasses, remember that they can be stylish as well. Choose the proper frame.

> **TIP:** When you buy sunglasses, they should have ultra-violet protection. Your eyes can be damaged by invisible ultra-violet rays.

Belts and Suspenders

Belts are intended to keep your pants up, but that doesn't mean thay can't look good too. Most common are neutral colored leather belts (black, brown, and gray) and cloth belts. Some pants come with their own cloth belt which you can use on other pants, if it matches. When in doubt, a reversible brown/black leather belt can usually match whatever you're wearing.

Suspenders come in and out of fashion all the time, so they're good to have. Thin suspenders that match your pants are the best way to go.

Ties

A good selection of stylish ties is a must for every guy's wardrobe. The right tie can make an otherwise dull outfit exciting. The rules for matching ties are by and large the same as the rules for matching clothes. Ties with busy patterns work best on solid colored shirts. They look best when they match your pants, or some color in your shirt.

Ties are versatile and can be worn several different ways; loose, with the top shirt-button open, or snug, with the button closed. The front flap of the tie should be slightly longer than the tail, and should just about reach your belly-button when you stand up straight.

Shoes

Dress shoes are generally made of leather and usually come in neutral colors, so they will go with everything. Take care to keep them well polished. Dress shoes look really awful if they're not well cared for.

There are all kinds of casual shoes. Topsiders are probably the most common, because they're multi-purpose. They can look good when you're dressed up or just going to the beach.

It used to be that everyone wore sneakers to play sports. Now the makers of athletic shoes have turned footwear into an art and science. There are all kinds of shoes to match all kinds of tastes and activities.

Whatever type of sports shoes you buy, remember to check quality against price. Some inexpensive sports shoes may be a good buy, but others may just look good, and be poorly made. Bad shoes will fall apart more quickly than anything else in your wardrobe. Some inexpensive sports shoes may look like they're made of leather, but are actually made of plastic or vinyl. They won't last as long.

A Word on Socks

Dress socks come in many colors. Most people choose a neutral. Match the clothes or shoes you're wearing. The object is to provide a visual bridge between your shoes and pants.

When exercising, wear white sweat socks. They absorb sweat the best. Be stylish by matching the stripes in the socks to the color of the sports clothes you're wearing. The smell of some guy's sneakers could wipe out the population of a small city. Change your socks daily — more often if you're really active.

"C'mon, Mom, it's only an earring..."

There are some guys who wear so much jewelry, they could double as lightning rods. For guys, jewelry should be kept at a minimum. A watch, a ring, a simple necklace that's not as fat as a rope, maybe a man's wristlet is all you really need. Keep it simple!

There's a trend in fashion these days that has caused a big stir. Earrings. A boy wearing an earring is a bit more extreme than anything else discussed in this book. Most parents dread the thought of their son wearing an earring, because they see it as one step before getting a mohawk.

When you wear an earring, you're making a statement, and people will judge you for it. Adults may automatically see you as rebellious and troublesome. An earring could even alienate some of your friends. If you're thinking of getting your ear pierced, take time to think about it. Make sure it's something you really want to do. You may find that, in the long run, it causes more problems than it's worth.

ONE FINAL WORD

We all know that looking good is important, but that's only part of a bigger picture. The outside should only be a reflection of what's going on inside. A change of clothes or hairstyle won't change your life, so don't expect it to. If you're down on yourself, it will still show no matter what you wear; a change has to come from the inside, not outside. On the other hand, if you feel really good about yourself and have a good outlook on life, that will show too, no matter what you wear!

BIBLIOGRAPHY

"Attention to Detail," Gentleman's Quarterly. January 1988, p. 110.

"A Cut Above," Esquire. March 1988, pps. 164-166.

Fit or Fat, Covert Bailey. Houghton Mifflin Company, Boston

"The Baseball Cap," Esquire. February 1987, p 19.

"Child Achievers," Child Magazine. June 1988, p 51.

"Cut Loose," Gentleman's Quarterly. June 1988, p. 196.

Clothes and the Man, Alan Flusser. Villard Books, New York.

"Great Summer Haircuts," Gentleman's Quarterly. June 1987, p. 155.

Dressing Right, Charles Hix. St. Martin's Press, New York.

The New Teenage Body Book, Kathy McCoy and Charles Wibbelsman, M.D. The Body Press, Los Angeles.

Guy Talk, Neal Shusterman. Weekly Reader Books, Columbus.

"Total Summer Fitness," Gentleman's Quarterly. May 1988, p. 209.

INDEX